Wonders of the Ocean

Earth is sometimes called the "blue planet" because ocean waters cover two-thirds of its surface! Spreading across our blue planet are five large oceans and seven smaller seas. From shallow coastal regions to the deepest waters, the world's oceans are home to many animals and plants.

Millions of different fish swim in the oceans, from little clownfish to huge sharks. Many other animals live there as well, including polar bears, sea otters, clams, crabs, and sea turtles.

There are lots of birds by the oceans, too. Some are great flyers, like the albatross. Others, like penguins, "fly" underwater instead of in the air.

This poster project shows ocean habitats with stickers for some of the creatures who can be found in each one. Read about the different habitats, then put the stickers in the part of the ocean where they belong.

Make a Giant
OCEAN POSTER

Learn about the wonders of the ocean by putting together a beautiful poster to hang on your wall! Use the stickers to complete the ocean scene on the poster.

1. Unfold your poster and lay it flat on a table.

2. Pick a sticker and find the outline on the poster that matches it.

3. Place the sticker on its spot on the poster. Watch your ocean scene come alive as you add more stickers!

4. Hang your finished poster on your wall. How many ocean creatures can you name?

Where do CREATURES of the OCEAN live?

THE FROZEN POLES

In the North and South Poles, a surprising number of animals have found ways to survive the harsh, icy environments.

- Polar bear
- Narwhal
- Beluga whale
- Walrus
- Arctic tern
- Emperor penguin
- Blue whale
- Krill
- Lantern fish
- Leopard seal

HIGH SEAS

Out on the open ocean, far from land, the high seas are the largest habitat on Earth.

- Albatross
- Leatherback sea turtle
- Gray whale
- Tuna
- Great white shark
- Spinner dolphin

MANGROVE FOREST

Mangroves are the only trees in the world that can live in saltwater. Their tangled roots provide shelter and feeding grounds for many interesting animals.

- Horseshoe crab
- Mudskipper
- Jellyfish
- Manatee
- Spotted eagle ray

INTO THE DEEP

The earth's oceans are deeper than Mount Everest, the tallest mountain on the planet. A huge variety of marine creatures live in these mysterious, dark waters.

- Frilled shark
- Fangtooth fish
- Vampire squid
- Dumbo octopus
- Viperfish
- Anglerfish

KELP FOREST

Kelp is a type of seaweed that grows in long strands from the ocean floor. Big clumps of kelp form underwater forests along many coastlines.

- Sea otter
- Sunflower sea star
- Sea lion
- Sea urchin
- Kelp rockfish
- Loggerhead sea turtle

ROCKY SEASHORE

Shallow waters at the ocean's edge provide shelter and food to many different animals and plants. The movement of the tide in and out creates pools in rocky areas.

- Common limpet
- Barnacle
- Sea squirt
- Sea anemone
- Sea star
- Hermit crab
- Octopus

CORAL REEF

A reef is made up of thousands of tiny animals called coral polyps that grow very slowly to create a large structure. Coral reefs provide habitat to 25 percent of all marine life on Earth.

- Clownfish
- Parrotfish
- Triggerfish
- Moray eel
- Crown-of-thorns sea star
- Giant clam
- Sea cucumber
- Lionfish
- Hammerhead shark
- Blue shark

NOTE: *Many of these animals travel great distances and can be found in different areas of the ocean at different times.*

Krill

THE FROZEN POLES, continued

Beluga whale

Walrus

Leatherback sea turtle

Tuna

Gray whale

Spinner dolphin

HIGH SEAS

Albatross

Great white shark

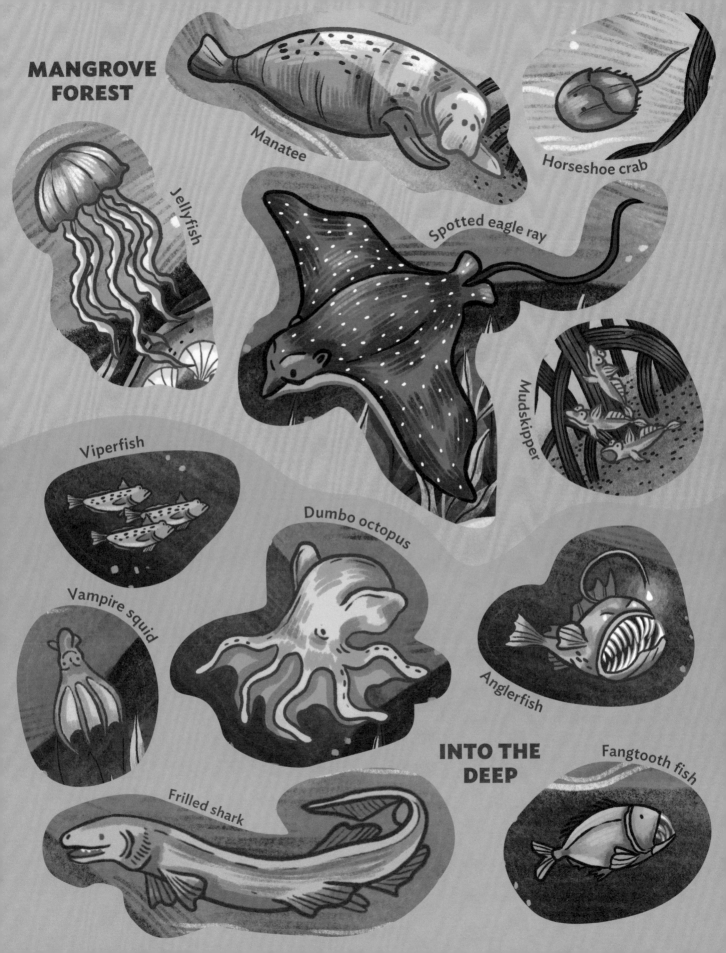

MANGROVE FOREST

Manatee

Horseshoe crab

Jellyfish

Spotted eagle ray

Mudskipper

Viperfish

Dumbo octopus

Vampire squid

Anglerfish

INTO THE DEEP

Fangtooth fish

Frilled shark

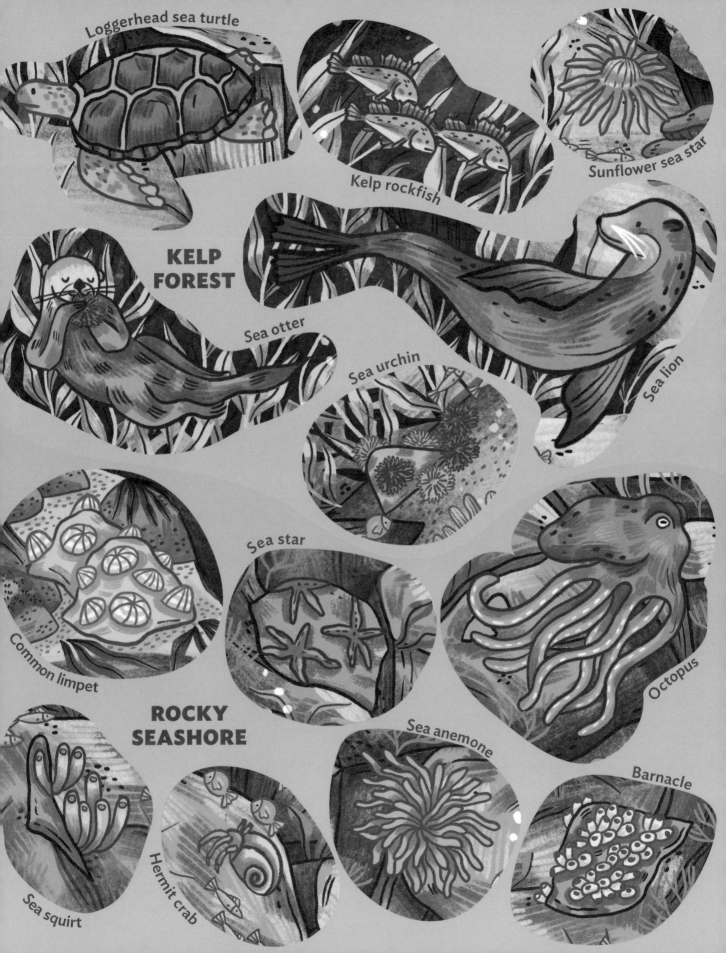

Loggerhead sea turtle

Kelp rockfish

Sunflower sea star

KELP FOREST

Sea otter

Sea lion

Sea urchin

Common limpet

Sea star

Octopus

ROCKY SEASHORE

Sea anemone

Barnacle

Sea squirt

Hermit crab

Moray eel

Lionfish

Sea cucumber

Triggerfish

CORAL REEF

Hammerhead shark

Clownfish

Giant clam

Parrotfish

Crown-of-thorns sea star

Blue shark